JOHN GOWER

reproduced from an engraving by GEORGE VERTUE, 1727
British Museum

GOWER
AND
LYDGATE

by

DEREK PEARSALL

Edited by Geoffrey Bullough

PUBLISHED FOR
THE BRITISH COUNCIL
AND THE NATIONAL BOOK LEAGUE
BY LONGMANS, GREEN & CO

LONGMANS, GREEN & CO LTD
Longman House, Burnt Mill, Harlow, Essex

*Associated companies, branches and
representatives throughout the world*

First published 1969
© Derek Pearsall 1969

*Printed in Great Britain by
F. Mildner & Sons, London, EC1*

Some dates in the life of John Gower

c.1330   John Gower born, of a landed family originating from Yorkshire, but soon to move to Kent.

c.1342   Geoffrey Chaucer born.

1365–74   Gower involved in complex estate transactions in Kent. He appears to have been a speculative investor in real estate, perhaps with some legal training.

1377   Death of Edward III. Accession of Richard II, aged ten.

1376–9   *Mirour de l'Omme*

1378   Chaucer gave him power of attorney while away in Italy.

1379–82   *Vox Clamantis*

1381   Peasants' Revolt.

1382   Estates in Norfolk and Suffolk acquired and immediately leased.

1386   Chaucer dedicated *Troilus* to Gower and Strode.

1386–90   *Confessio Amantis*

1392–3   Revised dedication of *Confessio* to Henry of Lancaster, Earl of Derby.

1393   Henry of Lancaster (the future Henry IV) presented him with a ceremonial collar.

1398   Jan. 25 Married Agnes Groundolf at St Mary Magdalene in Southwark. Resident in lodgings in the Priory of St Mary Overey in Southwark (where he had probably been living in semi-retirement since 1377).

1399   Deposition of Richard II.
Oct. 13 Coronation of Henry IV.
Nov. 21 Grant by the king of two pipes of Gascony wine annually to 'the King's Esquire John Gower'.

1400   Oct. 25 Death of Chaucer.

1402   Becomes blind: Gower had long been an invalid—probably Agnes was his nurse.

1408   Aug. 15 Gower's will attested.
Oct. 24 Will proved: to be buried in the Priory Church of St Mary Overey (afterwards St Saviour's Church, Southwark, now Southwark Cathedral).

Some dates in the life of John Lydgate

c.1370   Born at Lydgate, a small village in Suffolk.

1385   Entered abbey of Bury St Edmunds, Suffolk, as a novice.

1389   Admitted to minor orders.

1397   Ordained priest.

c.1400–10   Probably composing courtly poems and love-allegories, and the *Life of Our Lady*.

1406–8   Training at Benedictine school (Gloucester Hall) in Oxford.

1412–20   *Troy-book*, commissioned by Prince Henry.

1413   Death of Henry IV. Accession of Henry V.

1420–22   *Siege of Thebes*

1422   Death of Henry V. Accession of Henry VI, aged nine months. Humphrey, Duke of Gloucester, Regent in England; Duke of Bedford, Regent in France.

1423–34   Lydgate Prior of Hatfield Broadoak, Essex (but resident only 1423–6).

1426   In Paris, writing a poetical pedigree of Henry VI for the Earl of Warwick.

1426–8   *Pilgrimage of the Life of Man*, translated for the Earl of Salisbury. Probably in France, in official entourage of the Duke of Bedford.

1429   Coronation of Henry VI, celebrated in verse by Lydgate.

1430–8   *Fall of Princes*, commissioned by Humphrey of Gloucester.

1432   Henry VI's return to London after coronation in France; celebrated by Lydgate in his official capacity as 'court-poet'.

1434   Return to permanent residence at Bury St Edmunds.

1434   *Life of St Edmund*, written at request of Henry VI, on the occasion of his visit to Bury.

1435   Death of Bedford: marks final decline of English fortunes in France.

1439   *Life of St Albon*

1445   Verses for entry of Margaret, Henry VI's queen, into London.

1447   Trial and death of Gloucester.

c.1449   Death of Lydgate. Buried in the abbey at Bury St Edmunds.

JOHN GOWER

THE head of John Gower's effigy, on his tomb in St Saviour's Church, Southwark, rests upon three books, the *Speculum Meditantis*, the *Vox Clamantis*, and the *Confessio Amantis*, but his reputation as an English poet rests upon the last of these, the other two poems being in French (Anglo-French, to be precise, which differed somewhat from continental French) and in Latin respectively. That Gower wrote in three languages should not surprise us: French was the first language of the English upper classes until the middle of the fourteenth century, and the court language of Edward III and Richard II till the end of the century, while Latin was, and remained, the universal language of learning and serious literature. Gower has been reproached for lacking Chaucer's splendid certainty of Englishness, as if the three-fold phasing of his poetic output were a timid hedging of bets on posterior fame, a safe but unspectacular investment. But Chaucer's certainty was without precedent, and there is a logic in Gower's progress through the languages which reflects the age, as always, with great fidelity. The *Mirour de l'Omme* (called in Latin the *Speculum Meditantis* or *Speculum Hominis*) is a moral and didactic survey of the state of man, a handbook of sins, addressed to the thoughtful and literate laity as part of a long tradition of serious, practical, admonitory writing in Anglo-French. The *Vox Clamantis* is a calling to account of English society and government before the bar of posterity: its aim is to fix the age's infamy in a context of history, scripture and prophecy, and to do so in a language which will endure. The *Confessio Amantis*, however, is confessedly a relaxation from these strenuous moral endeavours, a blending of 'lore' and 'lust'—like Polonius, Gower could not help assuming a hortatory role—in a pattern of sober comedy. As he says, too much moralizing 'dulleth oft a mannes wit', and therefore,

> I wolde go the middel weie
> And wryte a bok betwen the tweie,

Somwhat of lust,[1] somewhat of lore,[2]
That of the lasse or of the more
Som man mai lyke of that I wryte:
And for that fewe men endite
In oure englissh, I thenke make
A bok for Engelondes sake.

(Prologue, 17–24)

In this poem Gower found, as if by chance, his natural voca-
tion as a polished and fluent verse narrator, and it is this
story-teller's gift which is our chief delight in reading Gower,
and his chief claim on our attention.

Yet it is not his only claim, nor is it separable from his role
as a moralist, for Gower's narratives, however divergent
and remote their sources, are staked out in a world of consis-
tent social and moral values, a world of civilized feelings,
which Gower can now define all the more effectively because he is writing out of imaginative sympathy and not
out of admonitory purpose. In some manuscripts of the
Vox Clamantis there is a picture illustrating some Latin verses
which begin:

Ad mundum mitto mea iacula, dumque sagitto.[3]

It portrays Gower as an old man, in a long gown, of worn
but resolute mien, in the act of shooting an arrow at the
round globe of the world. It is an image we should remember, of John Gower as the keeper of the nation's conscience
in a brilliant, violent and corrupt generation, for it is an
essential part of the whole man. Chaucer recognized this
when he dedicated his *Troilus and Criseyde* in 1386 to 'moral
Gower', along with 'philosophical Strode', though he may
not have realized how effectively he was entombing his
friend's poetic reputation by so doing. It is a fact that the
praise lavished by the fifteenth century on Gower, in which
he is formally acknowledged, with Chaucer and Lydgate, as
one of the three founders of English poetry, is not accom-
panied by the devotion and enthusiasm which Hoccleve

---

[1] pleasure.   [2] teaching.
[3] I hurl my darts at the world and I shoot my arrows.

and Lydgate, for instance, display for Chaucer, or Hawes for Lydgate. Although the *Confessio* was put out in printed form in 1483, and again in 1532 and 1554, and although both Shakespeare (in *Pericles*) and Ben Jonson (in his *Grammar*) show knowledge of his work, it was generally Gower's fate to remain admired but unread, then to be forgotten (no further edition appeared until 1810), and further to suffer the slings and arrows of Coleridge, Lowell and Jusserand before being salvaged by having his morality thrown overboard. Yet, as we have seen, the *Confessio* does not stand alone, and some account of Gower's other work is needed before we can see it in perspective.

The *Mirour de l'Omme* (the 'Mirror of Man') survives incomplete in a single manuscript as a poem of 28,603 lines, in a difficult octosyllabic twelve-line stanza. It is in three parts: the first, occupying 18,000 lines, is a schematic analysis of the Seven Deadly Sins and the opposed seven virtues, each sub-divided into five aspects; the second part shows how Sin has corrupted the world, by examining the different ranks of society—clergy, secular rulers, knights, lawyers, merchants, craftsmen, tradesmen and labourers; the third part outlines the way to amendment through repentance and through the intercession of the Virgin, whose life is recounted. The work as a whole is impressively organized as a mechanical structure, and is sustained by the medieval passion for a comprehensive schematization of the moral nature of things, for a *Summa*. Everything is related to the microcosmic combat of Passion and Reason in fallen man, and this combat is reflected in the corruption of nature and society, just as the cathedral is an image of the risen body of man and an image too of the structure of medieval thought, itself a 'cathedral of ideas'. Gower is dealing with the same raw material as Chaucer and Langland—hardly a detail of Chaucer's Monk or Friar is absent here—but, although he can demonstrate a lively satiric observation, as when he speaks of the vintner whose samples are so different from what you actually buy (26,070), and who seems to be able to get a dozen different exotic wines from the same cask (26,101), Gower always moves towards the general and the abstract. Over some maps one can place a transparent grid so as to make plotting of reference easier: Gower places a moral grid over the map of human experience and reads it through that. Every human action is plotted on this grid and given a reference in terms of the enumerated scheme of vices and virtues. Chaucer knew this grid too, but he was not afraid to remove it and look at the map of experience in itself—though he was glad enough to put it back when he had looked hard and long enough, as the Epilogue to the *Troilus* and the Retraction show. Thus Gower, unlike Chaucer, can rarely get beyond the schematic truth of 'Les bons sont bons, les mals sont mals,' (25,225) except, as we shall see, when he is telling a story. Gower is not a philosophical poet, like Boethius or Jean de Meun, the continuator of the *Roman de la Rose*; his mind is not stirred and his imagination is not moved by ideas, concepts or the majestic processes of reason. For Gower, truth is a castle, a castle under constant attack whose walls are crumbling and showing fissures. It is his duty, not to make daring exploratory forays into the hinterland of experience, but to shore up these fragments against the world's ruin.

In the *Vox Clamantis* ('The Voice of One Crying'), a poem of 10,265 lines, extant in eleven manuscripts, Gower associates himself explicitly, by his title, with the Messianic prophets, Isaiah and John the Baptist, and, in the Prologue to Book I, with that other John of the Apocalypse. His vision is of a society rushing onward towards its doom, driven like Gadarene swine by the sins of the flesh, while God's wrath burns hidden, and his call is to the people to repent before the inevitable destruction. Book II, the original opening book, offers a *Credo*, and, dismissing the idea that Fortune is the author of the world's unhappiness and instability, asserts the essential moral responsibility of Man and the subservience of Fortune and Nature to the just man (nothing better illustrates the meaninglessness of *experience*, in the medieval scheme, in comparison with moral *truth*).

Having placed man firmly in the dock, Gower now proceeds to arraign him, in the next four books, much as in the *Mirour*, by analyzing at length the corruption of all estates of society. There is some powerful writing here, especially against the clergy, often reminiscent of *Piers Plowman* and the clerical portraits of the *Prologue to the Canterbury Tales*, though praise of his satiric 'realism', as of Chaucer's and Landland's, is perforce inhibited by the fact that much of their material is conventional. Gower also displays an extravagance of rhetoric, as in the description of woman's seductiveness (V. 79ff), and a savage Roman obscenity of wit as in the account of the priest's return to 'school' (III. 1,417ff; also IV. 603,861), which suggest something of the imaginative and verbal licence which Latin provided, when the simple innocence of the laity was not in danger of being corrupted. Book VI, after dealing with lawyers, turns to the young king and exhorts him to rule with justice and honour, using his father, the Black Prince, as his exemplar. A later revision of this passage (like Langland, Gower was a constant reviser) substitutes stern and menacing reproof for exhortation. Book VII introduces the Statue of Nebuchadnezzar's dream, with its head of gold, breast of silver, belly of brass, and feet of iron and clay, as an apocalyptic allegory of the successively degenerating ages of the world. We are now, says Gower, in the age of iron and clay, of hard-hearted avarice and fleshly lust—indicted as *Gallica peccata* ('the French sins', i.e. the cult of fashionable adultery). The wretchedness of the world is contrasted with God's original purpose for mankind, and Gower's favourite image of the microcosm is given a macabre twist in the comparison of worldly corruption to the corruption of the body after death, in their relation to the indulgence of particular sins (e.g. 848). The poem ends with a *Memento Mori*, visions of Hell, and a call to repent.

The most interesting part of the *Vox*, however, is Book I, added after the Peasants' Revolt of 1381 had provided Gower and his England with a foretaste of Apocalypse.

After a brilliant and luxuriant description of terrestrial paradise, as if to symbolize the bounty of Nature now corrupted by man, the poet, in a dream, sees the mob running wild, metamorphosed into animals, engaged in an orgy of destruction, looting and rape. London is sacked, the Archbishop of Canterbury martyred, in a riot of violent, highly charged imagery and classical allusion, and with the grossest distortion of historical truth. The Revolt certainly disturbed Gower, but it was a godsend to him as a fulfilment of his prophecies and as a way of getting his poem off to an explosive start.

Late in his life, Gower added a sequel to the *Vox*, called the *Cronica Tripertita* (the 'Three-part Chronicle'), in which Richard II is finally exposed and condemned. The first part, *opus humanum*, describes the brave resistance of Gloucester and the Lords Appellant to Richard's hateful tyranny; the second, *opus inferni*, recounts the treacherous murder of Gloucester and other of the king's infamies; the third, *opus in Cristo*, describes the deposition of Richard and the accession of Henry IV as something, allowing for poetic exaggeration, akin to a secular Second Coming.

There are other minor Latin poems, but it is time to turn now to the *Confessio Amantis* ('The Lover's Confession'). The poem was begun about 1386, and Gower tells us that it sprang from a suggestion of King Richard, whom he met on the Thames one day, that he should write 'som newe thing'. Perhaps the King was tired of being lectured by the stern old moralist—at any rate, Gower's response, in 33,444 lines of octosyllabic couplet (49 MSS), was above and beyond even a sovereign's call to duty. The poem was completed by 1390, but in 1393 Gower, now totally disgusted with Richard, revised him out of the Prologue and substituted a dedication to Henry, in whom he recognized, even at this early date, England's man of Destiny. This was not Gower's only revision of the *Confessio*: in another, a passage in the Epilogue in praise of Chaucer was excised. Venus addresses the poet Gower:

And gret wel Chaucer whan ye mete,
As mi disciple and mi poete:
For in the floures of his youthe
In sondri wise, as he wel couthe,[1]
Of Ditees[2] and of songes glade,
The whiche he for mi sake made,
The lond fulfild is overal . . .

(VIII. 2,941-7)

Such a change, in view of the long-standing and well-authenticated friendship of the two poets, could hardly have been accidental. Explanations are speculative: it may be that Gower took offence at Chaucer's good-humoured sniping in the Introduction to the *Man of Law's Tale*, where he makes some ironical play of moral Gower's fondness for tales of incest (77–89), though the irony is directed more at the lawyer's ignorance than at Gower.[3] There are two further passages in the *Tale* (1,009, 1,086) which may or may not be playfully critical of Gower's telling of the same tale of Constance in Book II of the *Confessio*. A touchy man could have taken them seriously. Perhaps, though, Gower was more generally disillusioned with Chaucer because of the direction which the *Canterbury Tales* seemed to be taking in these later years of Chaucer's life. The *Miller's Tale* and the others must have looked to Gower like an appeal to the basest tastes of the public and a betrayal of the high cause of poetry.

The intention of the *Confessio*, as we have seen, is to blend entertainment with instruction, but Gower cannot descend from the pulpit so readily, and in the Prologue therefore he recapitulates familiar moral themes—the corruption of the world, analysed through the three estates, the moral responsibility of man, the insignificance of Fortune, the microcosmic relation of man and Nature, the decay of the age and the coming destruction, embodied again in the allegory of Nebuchadnezzar's dream. In Book I, however, Gower deftly shifts his ground:

[1] knew how.   [2] poems.   [3] See Bibl.

> I may noght strecche up to the hevene
> Min hand, ne setten al in evene
> This world, which evere is in balance:
> It stant noght in my sufficance
> So grete thinges to compasse,
> Bot I mot lete it overpasse
> And treten upon othre thinges.
> Forthi the Stile of my writinges
> From this day forth I thenke change
> And speke of thing is noght so strange,[1]
> Which every kinde hath upon honde,[2]
> And whereupon the world mot stonde,[3]
> And hath don sithen it began,
> And schal whil there is any man;
> And that is love, of which I mene
> To trete, as after schal be sene.
>
> (I. 1–16)

But it is *reculer pour mieux sauter*. The controlling theme of the *Prologue* is of division, in man's own nature and in society, as the source of all strife and all evil, and the transition to the theme of love is a natural one. For Gower, love is a principle of existence, a blind natural force, in itself neither good nor evil, but providing the strongest motive to good or evil and therefore for the display of man's moral nature. He recognizes that talk of love and tales of love are interesting in themselves, but he recognizes too that this interest can be used to probe human behaviour in its most vulnerable and sensitive areas, that is, where man is passionately *involved*, and so quicken moral receptivity. He is not teaching an amorous morality or code of sexual behaviour, but evolving patterns of rational morality by reference to sexual passion. There is nothing artificial here, since the art of 'fyn lovynge', as Chaucer calls it, and as he and others embody it in their writings, is not so very different from the art of fine living:

> Thus wolde Love, yheried be his grace,

[1] difficult.   [2] which controls every creature.   [3] must stand.

That Pride, Envye, and Ire, and Avarice
He gan to fle, and everich other vice.
(*Troilus* III. 1804-6)

Like man in general, the lover must eschew the deadly sins,
even lechery, for the characteristic theme which Gower
develops in the *Confessio* is of the control of blind passion
through the exercise of reason, and of marriage as the true
goal of 'fyn lovynge':

It sit[1] a man be weie of kinde[2]
To love, bot it is noght kinde[3]
A man for love his wit to lese.
(*Confessio* VII. 4,297-9)

The dramatic scheme of the *Confessio* is for Gower to
imagine himself as a lover—the fiction is openly and half-
mockingly contrived—and to appeal to Venus for respite
from the pain of Cupid's fiery dart. Venus, before granting
his request, demands that he should be shriven by Genius,
the Priest of Love, so as to prove his worth and virtue as a
lover. Genius is taken from the *Roman de la Rose*, but he
plays a completely new part in the *Confessio*: in a superficial
sense, he is a product of the fashionable habit of applying
religious terms to love, as is the idea of a 'lover's confession',
but essentially he represents the conscience of Love, and
comes to represent, through the poem, the conscience of the
lover. His technique is to go through the Seven Deadly
Sins, dividing each into five aspects (it sometimes seems that
Gower had only one poem to write, but had to write it in
three languages), to analyze each in both its general and
amorous manifestations, to question the lover as to his guilt,
and to offer exemplary stories. The scheme, which is
evidently derived from that of the penitential manual,
allows him to speak with great freedom and to cover the
whole range of human behaviour—sometimes, indeed, he
gives but scant attention to the lover's timid confessions in
his pursuit of the larger truths. Gower makes some wry

[1] befits.   [2] in the way of nature.   [3] according to nature.

comedy out of this: when Genius is expatiating on the evils of sloth, in particular of *lachesse* (procrastination), the lover ruefully interjects that he never has the *chance* to be late for a date, because his lady never gives him one (IV. 271); and when Genius is speaking of Idleness, the lover declares his assiduity in the service of love, though, as he admits, it never seems to get him anywhere.

> Al is bot ydel ate laste.
>
> (IV. 1758)

It is idle, but is it idleness? The lover has too a mind of his own, though somewhat overawed in the presence of his shrift-father. When Genius tells the story of Phebus and Daphne as a warning against over-hastiness, the lover thanks him for his advice, but roundly asserts that so long as he sees his lady is no tree, he will continue to pursue her (III. 1,730). Again, the Priest's advocacy of prowess in arms as a way to win his lady's heart cuts no ice with him at all:

> What scholde I winne over the Se,
> If I mi ladi loste at hom?
>
> (IV. 1,664-5)

When questioned about the sin of ingratitude, the lover suggests with some trepidation that it is his lady who is ungrateful, half-expecting the thunders which proceed to roll about his head (V. 5,210).

The development of this dry and rueful comedy of the lover is one of the achievements of the *Confessio*. It is not sufficient to give the poem the organic quality of growth of the *Canterbury Tales*; it remains a mechanical structure, a continuing argument rather than a drama, but the dramatic scheme gives the whole poem a buoyancy which other collections of exemplary tales, like the *Gesta Romanorum* or even the *Legend of Good Women*, lack. Many delicate touches enliven the character of the lover for us, and a number of longer passages portray his 'service' with fine, gentle sympathy and a kind of wistfulness. We hear of his eagerness to please his lady, how he conducts her to church:

> Thanne is noght al mi weie in vein,
> Somdiel I mai the betre fare,
> What I, that mai noght fiele hir bare,
> Mai lede hire clothed in myn arm.
>
> (IV.   1,138–41)

But the moment of delight is lost in longing:

> Ha, lord, hou sche is softe,
> How sche is round, hou sche is smal![1]
>
> (IV.   1,146–7)

At home, his eyes follow her everywhere: when she takes up her embroidery:

> Than can I noght bot muse and prie
> Upon hir fingres longe and smale.
>
> (IV.   1,176–7)

Sometimes he will play with her little dog, or with her caged birds, partly to please her, partly because they are at least something of hers.   Elsewhere, he tells of his joy in her presence, especially when dancing gives him the excuse to hold her hand:

> With such gladnesse I daunce and skippe,
> Me thenkth I touche noght the flor;
> The Ro, which renneth on the Mor,
> Is thanne noght so lyht as I.
>
> (IV.   2,784–7)

At other times he plays 'chance' or 'love-questions' with her, or reads *Troilus* to her; when he has to leave, he tarries at the door, sometimes comes back for something he says he has forgotten, and when he gets back to his own bedchamber torments himself with thoughts of her:

> Into hire bedd myn herte goth,
> And softly takth hire in his arm
> And fieleth hou that sche is warm,
> And wissheth that his body were
> To fiele that he fieleth there.
>
> (IV.   2,884–8)

[1] slender.

In the end he sleeps: 'Bot that [what] I dreme is noght of schep.' (IV. 2,894). This is not passion, but fine feeling refined to the point where it begins to bear a resemblance to that purification of the will which is the moralist's goal. The ending of the poem describes how Venus promises to heal him of his 'unsely jolif wo', and does so by urging that he should make a 'beau retret' in the face of advancing age:

> 'That which was whilom grene gras,
> Is welked[1] hey at time now.
> Forthi mi conseil is that thou
> Remembre wel hou thou art old.'
>
> (VIII.   2,436–9)

Famous lovers of the past gather round him, wondering at such frostbitten fires, and Cupid gropes his way towards him and pulls out the 'fyri Lancegay'. The poet begs shame-facedly to be excused from the court and Venus, giving him a necklace of black beads engraved 'por reposer' and advising him to return to his moral books, betakes her to her home, 'Enclosid in a sterred sky'. (VIII. 2,942). It is a strangely moving ending, of which C. S. Lewis writes with deep sympathy,[2] reaching out beyond love to age, to 'calm of mind, all passion spent', and to death. Like Chaucer, in the *Parlement of Foules*, Gower begins with a Prologue in which the barrenness of prescriptive morality is suggested, and then circles on the central passion and mystery of love, in which the good life is surely hidden somewhere, only to return in the end to his books. Chaucer, however, did find an answer in Book III of the *Troilus*: Gower's 'beau retret' is final.

The lover is sometimes used as a prompt for Genius, who has a penchant for general moral disquisition. Unguarded questions from the lover touch off long discourses on Gentillesse, on War and Peace, on false and true Religion (an especially long one, V. 747-1,959), while Book VII consists entirely of a systematic exposition of the bases of medieval knowledge, ending with an account of the duties of a good

---

[1] withered.   [2] See Bibl.

King, a 'Regiment of Princes', into which Gower concentrates all his political teaching. We must in these passages make some allowance for the medieval pressure towards encyclopaedism, but they are not, in the context of the whole work, irrelevant. They function, indeed, not as organic parts of a work of art with its own internal validity, but as the intellectual and informational basis of a programme which has external validity, that is, in its relation to the world of action. The *Confessio*, however, does in the end become something more than a programme, for it passes beyond prescription to a 'civilization of the heart', in which fine feeling, humane sensitivity and 'gentillesse' take over the role of conscience as the source of virtuous action. Sin is made to seem not so much deadly as stupid and *low*.

It is the stories above all in which this inner 'sentence' of the *Confessio* is embodied. There are 133 stories, totalling 17,213 lines, just over half the total for the poem, and ranging in length from *exempla* of a few lines to the 1,738 lines of 'Apollonius of Tyre' (Book VIII, not one of the best). The major sources are Ovid, especially the *Metamorphoses*, the *Roman de Troie* of Benoit de Sainte-Maure (completed in 1184), the Bible, and various medieval collections of tales such as the *Gesta Romanorum*. The best of these tales (e.g. 'Mundus and Paulina', 'Narcissus', 'Albinus and Rosemond', in Book I; 'Constantine and Silvester', II; 'Canacee', 'Pyramus and Thisbe', III; 'Pygmalion', 'Demephon and Phillis', 'Rosiphelee', 'Ceix and Alceone', 'Iphis and Anaxarathen', IV—much the best book; 'Jason and Medea', 'Adrian and Bardus', 'Tereus'; V, 'Lucrece', VII) display a consummate narrative skill, but they display also the way in which storytelling could release Gower's potential imaginative energy so that he could penetrate to the heart of and *realize* what elsewhere he could only *say*.

A simple demonstration is provided by the story of Constantine and Silvester, where Constantine's soliloquy (II. 3,243-73), rejecting the barbarous cure prescribed for his leprosy, represents in action the nobility of sentiment and

fineness of moral discrimination which Chaucer speaks of—
'Pitee renneth soone in gentil herte'. More complex is
Gower's version of Ovid's tale of Tereus. Ovid orches-
trates the tale with great sonority and decks it in all the rich
panoply of his rhetoric, dwelling on the details of Tereus'
mutilation of the raped Philomena (*Metamorphoses*, VI. 557)
and on the dismembering and cooking of Tereus' son by his
wife Procne and her sister (640–6). Every gruesome detail is
elaborated with a rich and wanton imagination, every speech
made the opportunity for a display of emotional rhetoric and
wit. Gower, however, turns what is essentially a simple,
indeed a meaningless tale of lust and revenge into a humanly
complex story in which the human emotions of outraged
maidenhood and outraged wifehood are given full expression and in which the whole action is related to a significant
context of good and evil. Tereus' crime is given a moral context in a finite world by Philomena's prayer to Jupiter (V.
5,741), and Procne's revenge is introduced by her prayers to
Venus (5,821), in which she asserts her own truth and fidelity
in marriage and the wrong done to her, and then to Apollo
(5,846), begging forgiveness for being the indirect cause of it.
At every point, Gower mutes the horror and invests the
action with sentiment of a morally discriminating kind, as if
the characters were operating in a received civilized environ-
ment and not in a world of inhuman passion and violence.
For all his artistic simplicity beside Ovid, Gower has a
notion of the complex meaningfulness of human behaviour,
of its 'pendulation' to use Auerbach's term, which Ovid
does not begin to approach. Chaucer, we may note in
passing, tells the story, in the *Legend of Good Women*, as if in
an idle daze.

In Pyramus and Thisbe the major change is the development of Thisbe's death-speech as a pathetic questioning of
justice and divine providence: 'Helas, why do ye with ous
so?' (III. 1,472). The word *deserve*, which occurs frequently
in Gower's retelling of classical stories, but not in Ovid, is an
index to the patterns of moral responsibility he draws out

from the tales. He makes nothing of the metamorphosis in
the Thisbe story (of the mulberry tree), but elsewhere, as in
the tale of Tereus and that of Ceix and Alceone, he uses the
transformation as a means to poeticize human values. So,
in the latter tale, he exploits the change of the dead husband
and wife into kingfishers, which in Ovid is simply strange
(*Met.* XI. 742), as an affirmation of the pathetically trium-
phant endurance of wifely fidelity:

> Hire wynges for hire armes tuo
> Sche tok, and for hire lippes softe
> Hire harde bile, and so ful ofte
> Sche fondeth[1] in hire briddes forme,
> If that sche mihte hirself conforme
> To do the plesance of a wif,
> As sche dede in that other lif:
> For thogh sche hadde hir pouer lore,[2]
> Hir will stod as it was tofore,
> And serveth him so as sche mai.
>
>   (IV.   3,106-15)

Chaucer, in the *Book of the Duchess*, has nothing of this—it is
not, indeed, to his purpose—and in other respects Gower's
telling of the tale is more skilful than Chaucer's. Everywhere, Gower invests his women with humanity and pathos,
as in the story of Lucrece, where he dwells at length on
Lucrece's openness and hospitality towards her treacherous
guest—an episode which Chaucer omits entirely in the
Legend of Good Women—and portrays her actions after the
rape as possessing something of the deliberate ordained
quality of a being who has already passed beyond the world,
like Clarissa (VII. 4,996–5,011). So with Medea, who, instead of being harried and lectured at every turn, as was the
medieval moralist's wont, is treated with great sympathy,
coming vividly alive when her maid brings news of Jason's
exploits:

> Sche tolde hire ladi what sche wiste,[3]
> And sche for joie hire Maide kiste.
>
>   (V.   3,799–800)

<hr>

[1] tries.   [2] lost her power.   [3] knew.

Something of the imaginative release which story-telling gave Gower is indicated by the tale of Canacee (Book III), where incest—unmentionable even to Chaucer—is viewed with a sober and touching lack of outrage as the natural outcome of blind instinctive passion, and where the moral reproof is directed against the father's uncomprehending wrath.

Some of Gower's success with the classical stories is due to his ruthlessness, his readiness to throw overboard the many-storied richnesses of antiquity in favour of a finite moral pattern, which in turn is reinforced by a uniformity of social setting. Ambiguities, fruitful or otherwise, are removed, and a clear story-line emerges, often with complete redirection of the original material to a new purpose. The stories of Jason and Medea, and of Paris and Helen, are examples of Gower's skill in cutting the antique moorings and isolating the tellable tale, akin to Malory's technique in handling the polyphonic or interwoven Arthurian narratives. Sometimes, of course, the classical material is intractable to Gower's purposes: there was not much, for instance, that the Christian moralist could make of the story of Orestes (Book III). Sometimes, too, the overt moral runs counter to the inner sense of the story. 'Pyramus and Thisbe', for instance, is ostensibly an exemplum against irrational haste, and at one point the story of Troilus and Criseyde is referred to as proof that no good can come of flirting in church (V. 7,599). What we can assume is that Gower would have come to some less trivial conclusion in actually *telling* the tale.

Comparison between Gower and Chaucer as narrative artists favours the former until we come to the *Canterbury Tales*, where the dramatic context provides the freedom Chaucer's imagination needs. Here, conventional themes, such as the sermon on the sins of the tavern in the *Pardoner's Tale* or the anti-feminist material of the *Wife of Bath's Prologue*, can be placed dramatically off-centre so as to explore a new dimension in narrative. Gower's Confessor, however, speaks with a generalized, impersonal, 'European' voice, from a calm centre of experience, and at times he has the kind of dullness of someone who speaks good sense *all* the time. Even the simplest of the *Canterbury Tales*, such as the *Physician's Tale* (corresponding to Gower's 'Appius and Virginia', VII. 5,131) and the *Manciple's Tale* ('Phebus and Cornide', III. 782—Chaucer's tale may contain some mockery of Gower here[1]), have a memorableness which Gower's versions lack, while the *Man of Law's Tale* is richer at every point than Gower's tale of Constance (II. 587). The truest measure of Chaucer's greatness, however, is in his treatment of a story analogous to Gower's tale of Florent (I. 1,407) in the *Wife of Bath's Tale*. By any normal standards, Gower's realization of the story is much superior to Chaucer's: he actually describes the hag, which seems important to an appreciation of Florent's dilemma; he portrays Florent with great humanity—how he rides away when she first lays down her terms, then drifts back, how he comforts himself with the thought that she cannot live long, how at the court he tries various other answers just in case they will get him off the hook, how he smuggles her unseen into his castle. Throughout he behaves with scrupulous honesty and honour, and the final disenchantment of the hag depends partly upon this. Chaucer, however, puts the knight in the wrong from the first by making the offence a rape, and subtly re-aligns the story and the question so that the knight gets no chance to choose whether to behave honourably or not. The very *Tale* itself is thus a demonstration of woman's right to sovereignty. When Chaucer is ploughing a rich furrow like this, comparison is less favourable to Gower.

One quality of the *Confessio* remains to be mentioned, without which it would be nothing: its verbal artistry. Enough has probably been quoted to show that Gower is indeed a poet, and a poet of the purest kind, one who seeks 'the best words in the best order' without fuss or display. Coleridge spoke of the 'neutral' style as Chaucer's special

[1] See Bibliography.

achievement, but he could well have used Gower as the exemplar of such a style, in which the language never draws attention to itself and in which the long verse paragraph is unfolded with a naturalness which seems—and this is the crown of art—artless. Yet it is a style which can rise, through its very integrity and purity, to the demands of the story, as with Jason's return with the Golden Fleece, where the very lines seem to embody life, joy and victory:

> The Flees he tok and goth to Bote,
> The Sonne schyneth bryhte and hote,
> The Flees of gold schon forth withal,
> The water glistreth overal.

> (V.   3731–4)

Brief quotation cannot truly represent Gower's artistry, for his technique is essentially one of diffusion. Perhaps the reader may be directed to the magnificent prayer of Cephalus to the Sun (IV. 3,197–3,237) as the supreme expression of Gower's art.

Late in life, old, blind and semi-invalid, Gower made a collection of fugitive pieces for a presentation volume for Henry IV. He included in it his only other English poem, the stately 'To King Henry IV, in Praise of Peace', some Latin verses, and the Cinkante[1] Balades. These last, whether they are actually the work of a man of seventy or whether they are youthful productions gathered for publication, represent the sweetest flowering of 'fyn lovynge'. They do not describe passion, in fact the idea that they embody a personal love-story is wholly erroneous: they are, rather, a pleasing arrangement of gentle and noble sentiments. Certainly, they surpass anything of the kind, in English or French, before the Elizabethans, and through them we hear a familiar voice speaking, graceful, calm, faintly wry, but perhaps, finally, reconciled: 'Amour s'acorde a nature et resoun'. (Balade 50).

---

[1] Fifty.

JOHN LYDGATE

John Lydgate is at once a greater and a lesser poet than John Gower. He is a greater poet because of his greater range and force: he has a much more powerful machine at his command. The sheer bulk of Lydgate's poetic output is prodigious, amounting as it does, at a conservative count, to about 145,000 lines. Life at the monastery of Bury St Edmund's, where he spent most of his life, gave him a leisure which many another poet might have envied, and enabled him to explore and establish every major Chaucerian genre, except such as were manifestly unsuited to his profession, like the *fabliau*. In the *Troy-book* (30,117 lines), an amplified translation of the Trojan history of the thirteenth-century Latin writer Guido della Colonna, commissioned by Prince Henry (later Henry V), he moved deliberately beyond the *Knight's Tale* and the *Troilus* and provides a full-scale epic. The *Siege of Thebes* (4,716 lines) is a shorter excursion in the same field of chivalric epic. The *Monk's Tale*, itself a brief catalogue of the vicissitudes of Fortune, gives a hint of what is to come in the massive *Fall of Princes* (36,365), which is also derived, though not directly, from Boccaccio's *De Casibus Virorum Illustrium*.[1] The *Man of Law's Tale*, with its rhetorical elaboration of apostrophe, invocation and digression in what is essentially a saint's legend, is the model for Lydgate's legends of *St Edmund* (3,693) and *St Albon* (4,734), both local monastic patrons, as well as for many shorter saints' lives, though not for the richer and more genuinely devout *Life of Our Lady* (5,932). The allegorical love-vision is represented in fine poems like the *Complaint of the Black Knight*, the *Flower of Courtesy*, a Valentine's day poem in praise of his lady, and the *Temple of Glass*, a highly stylized account of a decorous romantic courtship and there are many graceful shorter love-poems (that these are not autobiographical hardly needs demonstrating). *Reason and Sensuality*

---

[1] 'Concerning the Falls of Famous Men'.

(7,042) is a translation of the first part of a French poem called 'Les Echecs Amoureux',[1] in which Lydgate hit on a happy blend of moralistic and love allegory. The *Pilgrimage of the Life of Man* (24,832) is a good deal less happy, a moral allegory of a type which may have influenced Bunyan's *Pilgrim's Progress*. It is translated from a French poem by Guillaume de Deguileville, and, except for the curious literalness of its allegory, which has a weird Bosch-like quality at times, has no claim at all on our attention—significantly, it is in a genre for which Lydgate found no precedent in Chaucer. The moral beast-fable, which Chaucer transfigured into the *Nun's Priest's Tale*, is represented in the 'Churl and the Bird', a poem of some pith, in 'The Horse, Goose and Sheep', and in some poor versions of 'Isopes Fabules'.

Nor does this exhaust Lydgate's output. There are at least two genres in which he successfully exploits native non-Chaucerian traditions, the Marian hymn (there are minor examples in Chaucer), to which he brings an intensity and verbal luxuriance rare in English, and the gnomic moralizing poem, where by contrast he is consciously writing 'low style', without aureation or rhetorical elaboration, and achieves a pungent aphoristic compression in poems like 'That now is Hay some-tyme was Grase' and 'A Wicked Tunge wille sey Amys'. In addition there are a large number of occasional and informational pieces in verse. Lydgate was something of a professional court poet, and counted among his patrons not only Henry V but also Humphrey, Duke of Gloucester (for the *Fall*), the Earl of Salisbury (for the *Pilgrimage*), the Countess of Warwick (for a version of *Guy of Warwick*, traditionally regarded as his worst poem), and others. From time to time he would also receive commissions from Henry VI: the King's title being in question, Lydgate wrote verses on the *Title and Pedigree of Henry VI*, and for the pageant of *Henry VI's Triumphal Entry into London* he wrote what we should call now a souvenir pro-

---
[1] 'Love's Game of Chess'.

gramme. An 'Epithalamion for Gloucester' shows how skilfully Lydgate could handle intrinsically unpromising material. Often he was asked for little masques or 'mummings' for performance at convivial gatherings of such companies as the London Mercers and Goldsmiths, and these pieces have an importance in the history of dramatic literature which is only just being recognized. If such 'occasional' pieces as these have to be written, then Lydgate's are about as good as they can be within their unenviable limits. We have also to appreciate that poetry in the fifteenth century was expected to cover a much wider range of human needs and activities than it does now. There were no 'unpoetic' subjects, and consequently we find poems in the Lydgate canon on subjects for which we should now consult a history-book or encyclopaedia, or even a cookery-book or 'Family Doctor'. There is a 'Pageant of Knowledge', covering the same ground as Book VII of Gower's *Confessio*, a verse tabulation of the 'Kings of England', a 'Dietary' or guide to good health (Lydgate's most popular work, to judge by the number of extant manuscripts!), a 'Treatise for Laundresses', and a book of etiquette for young boys, 'Stans Puer ad Mensam', full of imperishable wisdom such as 'Pike nat thy nase' and 'With ful mouth speke nat, list thou do offence'. In the *Troy-book* and the *Fall*, too, the encyclopaedic tendency is always present: in the former, for instance, when describing the rebuilding of Ilium, he digresses at length, with only hints from his source, on the origin of chess, the value of *pi*, the nature of classical drama, and the Trojan sewage system (into which he incorporates the latest fifteenth century thinking on the subject), while the latter shows a strong inclination to become, at times, in its remorseless inventory of the victims of Fortune, a Dictionary of Universal Biography, since the only essential qualification for inclusion is to be dead.

All this, of course, swells the corpus of Lydgate's work enormously, and in a way that is essentially trivial by our standards. But we should be prepared to recognize the narrowing down that has taken place in the role of poetry and not blame Lydgate, though it is a human enough reaction, for having written so much. In a deeper sense, however, the massiveness of Lydgate's poetic production is an essential factor in our judgment of him, particularly in the two longest poems, the *Troy-book* and the *Fall*. A Lydgate anthology would be useful, but it can never truly represent him, just as quotation can never do him justice, for he achieves his most powerful effects over vast canvases. There is an ethos of the long poem, to which we, with our modern taste for compression and witty intensity, are not readily responsive, one in which the poetic effect is built up by sheer insistence and cumulative iteration. *Richard III* is not Shakespeare's best play, but it looks a lot better at the end of a cycle of three less good plays, and so too the *Troy-book* and the *Fall* depend for a vital part of their power on the colossal sense of panoramic perspective that they develop. Their very size, like that of the Pyramids, is their meaning.

In this sense, then, Lydgate is a greater poet than Gower. But he is a lesser poet too, for in the way in which the word is widely used nowadays he is not a poet at all. What we expect of a poem is that its total meaning should be locally embodied, that the very texture of the poem's language and style should be susceptible of the same kind of critical attention and should yield the same critical results as the whole poem. With Chaucer this is true, and with Gower too, but not with Lydgate, except in a special sense which we shall develop, for he is the great example in our literature of the *rhetorician*. Lydgate has little concern for and little knowledge of the ways in which poetry can release the potentialities of old words or recognize new ones (though he did introduce many words into the language), and his understanding of the function of metre in poetry is naive. He took over the decasyllabic couplet and the seven-line stanza ('rhyme royal') from Chaucer, but he seems to appreciate little of his master's handling of them. Instead of attending to the rhythmic counterbalance of syntactical and metrical patterns, and the weaving of line-patterns into a continuous paragraph-flow, Lydgate appears to have tabulated Chaucer's techniques of variation and then to have used these as metrical standards. In other words, instead of the subtle challenge of the variant to the staple, we have the insistence on the variant as if it were the staple, with the result that Lydgate's verse is full of lines deficient of a syllable at the beginning (the 'headless' line) and at the caesura (the 'broken-backed' line). Such lines, perfectly acceptable in the Chaucerian continuum, give to Lydgate's verse the rigidity which is its great defect. So his verse, with its lack of verbal and rhythmical sensitivity, is in its local texture often drab and bare, in just the same way that Hardy's prose can in itself be exasperating. But this of course is not disabling: a medieval tapestry, upon close investigation, looks coarse and drab, but withdraw to take in the full effect and the whole pattern emerges. It is now our task to investigate the kind of patterns that Lydgate's verse makes.

Medieval rhetorical teaching concerns itself almost exclusively with style, and dismisses 'invention' and structure very briefly. Invention is mainly a matter of expanding familiar material through 'common-places', like allowing a crystal to grow in solution, while structure is treated from a mechanical rather than a dynamic point of view. Medieval poems are characteristically built up on numerical schemes, like the interwoven patterns of three and ten in Dante's *Divine Comedy* and the Seven Deadly Sins in Gower, or are based on allegorical schemes, like the pilgrimage and the other-world journey, or, simplest of all, are inventories. The *Fall*, for instance, is essentially a catalogue, though suggestions of a pageant of the dead are carried over from Boccaccio. The relative neglect of invention and structure is due to the unstated assumption that the material of poetry is all 'given'—there is nothing new to be said—and that its form is implied in its very existence. There is no need for Lydgate to 'organize' the *Fall*, nor for Langland to 'organize' *Piers Plowman*, because the world and all that is in it are already allegorically patterned by their Christian world-view. The task of the poet therefore is not to explore modes of experience and behaviour but to decorate and amplify the infinitely familiar, and it is to decoration and amplification that the medieval rhetorics devote themselves. Geoffrey of Vinsauf, for instance, an early thirteenth century Anglo-Latin rhetorician, well known in England in the fourteenth and fifteenth centuries, lists in his *Poetria Nova* ('The New Poetry') eight forms of amplification (e.g. periphrasis, simile, apostrophe, digression, description), and it would be easy to illustrate how fully Lydgate, in the *Troy-book*, demonstrates these techniques. Amplification, in fact, is for Lydgate an ingrained habit of mind more than a technique. Comparison with his sources shows how consistently there operates in him a kind of total recall: each move forward disturbs an avalanche and, before further progress can be made, a mass of illustrations, examples, images and similes have to be shifted. From poem to poem the same stimulus triggers off the same response. The ideal, and Lydgate puts it very simply, is not one of compression and economy, but one of expansiveness:

> These ookis grete be nat doun ihewe
> First at a stroke, but bi long processe,
> Nor longe stories a woord may not expresse.
>
> (*Fall* I. 96–97)

Lydgate seems to delight sometimes in his power of synonymy, of saying something in as many words as possible without adding to the meaning of what is said. This, for instance, is what he makes of 'Constant dripping wears away a stone':

> The rounde dropis off the smothe reyn,
> Which that discende and falle from aloffte
> On stonys harde, at eye as it is seyn,
> Perceth ther hardnesse with ther fallyng offte,
> Al-be in touchyng, water is but soffte;
> The percyng causid be force nor puissance,
> But off fallyng be long continuance.
>
> (*Fall* II. 106–12)

Lydgate amplifies by reflex, except when consciously writing 'low style', and subjects even the little moral fable of the 'Two Merchants' to the usual barrage of invocation, apostrophe, exclamation and complaint, with digressions on medicine and Levantine geography for good measure.

Decoration is handled by the rhetoricians in terms of diction, where they recommend richness, aureation, ornate luxuriance above all, and in terms of the tropes, such as metaphor, and the figures, such as repetition in its various forms. The treatment of the figures is fully schematized and every possible stylistic configuration is classified and analysed. The image of style is as of some rich brocaded garment which is cast over the naked body of the matter, or as of a form of painting—where the term 'colours of rhetoric' lends itself readily to elaborate word-play. Thus Peleus attempts to use his powers of persuasion upon Jason:

> And gan with asour and with golde to peynte
> His gay wordys in sownynge glorious.
>
> (*Troy* I.   384–5)

Elsewhere, interpreting the painting image with the utmost literalness, Lydgate speaks of himself and other followers of Chaucer, the great master-rhetorician, 'Amonge oure englisch that made first to reyne The gold dewe-dropis of rethorik so fyne':

> Whan we wolde his stile counterfet,
> We may al day oure colour grynde and bete,
> Tempre our azour and vermyloun:
> But al I holde but presumpcioun.
>
> (*Troy* II.   4,715–18)

It is not merely an image for Lydgate: for him words are surfaces, colours, bright counters to be arranged in patterns, not instruments for penetrating reality. In some of his Marian poems, the language becomes so aureate and Latinized that it seems to lose touch with referents in reality and to exist solely as a form of hieratic symbolic ritual.

The figures of rhetoric too are extensively used by Lydgate,
in ways that suggest that he found in their formal patternings
a way of controlling the overwhelming luxuriance of his
verbal responses, and many of his best lines achieve their
effect through traditional artifice, as with the *chiasmus* in the
third line of this passage:

> Noble Pryncis, in your prosperite,
> On sodeyn chaungis set your remembraunce,
> Fresshnesse off floures, off braunchis the beute
> Have ai on chaung a tremblyng attendaunce.
>
> (*Fall* III.   2,199–2202)

Lydgate seems to have been struck by certain figured caden-
ces in Chaucer, such as the 'Who looketh lightly now but
Palamoun' sequence in the *Knight's Tale* (1,870), which he
imitates several times, and the 'Lo here' anaphora of the
Troilus (V. 1,849), whose echoes he tries to catch on at least
five occasions, as here:

> Lo her the fyne[1] of loveres servise!
> Lo how that Love can his servantis quyte!
> Lo how he can his feythful men dispise,
> To sle[2] the trwe men, and fals to respite!
>
> ('Black Knight'.   400–3)

Again and again he returns to the opening lines of the
Parlement of Foules, trying to capture that unforgettable
cadence*:

> Our liff heer short, off wit the gret dulnesse,
> The hevy soule troublid with travaile,
> And off memorie the glacyng brotilnesse . . .[3]
>
> (*Fall* III.   22–24)

Such imitation is Lydgate's sincerest tribute to Chaucer, more
convincing even than the many passages where he enlarges
on his master's praise and laments the inadequacy of his
followers:

[1] end, result.   [2] slay.   [3] transient frailty.
* The lyf so short, the craft so long to lerne.

We may assay for to countrefete
His gaye style, but it wyl not be;
The welle is drie, with the lycoure swete,
Bothe of Clye and of Caliope.[1]

('Flower of Courtesy'. 239-42)

The conventional affectation of modesty becomes here a genuine humility, and a recognition of the debt they owed him:

To God I pray, that he his soule have,
After whos help of nede I moste crave,
And sek his boke that is left behynde
Som goodly worde therin for to fynde,
To sett amonge the crokid lynys rude
Whiche I do write.

(*Troy* II. 4,701-6)

Lydgate knew Chaucer's work intimately, in particular the *Troilus*, the *Parlement* and the *Knight's Tale*, and these he echoes and quotes constantly. The other *Canterbury Tales* he knew less well, and his attempt to write a Canterbury-link in the Prologue to the *Siege of Thebes* (which he dramatizes as his own Canterbury tale) is rather clumsy, and shows, for instance, that he has got the Miller, the Pardoner and the Summoner hopelessly mixed up (32-5). However, the fact that he *tried* to lumber after his master is a sign of his devotion, for Lydgate would have found it difficult to justify or even to understand the *Tales* in the terms of the prevailing poetic of rhetorical sententiousness.

Lydgate's characteristic techniques can only be illustrated by extended quotation. The following is part of the nature-description from the opening of the *Black Knight*:

I rose anon, and thoght I wolde goon
Unto the wode, to her the briddes sing,
When that the mysty vapour was agoon,
And clere and feyre was the morownyng,
And dewe also lyk sylver in shynyng

[1] Clio and Calliope, Muses.

Upon the leves, as eny baume[1] suete,
Til firy Tytan with hys persaunt hete

Had dried up the lusty lycour nyw
Upon the herbes in the grene mede,
And that the floures of mony dyvers hywe
Upon her stalkes gunne[2] for to sprede,
And for to splayen out her leves on brede[3]
Ageyn the sunne, golde-borned[4] in hys spere[5],
That doun to hem cast hys bemes clere.

And by a ryver forth I gan costey[6],
Of water clere as berel or cristal,
Til at the last I founde a lytil wey
Towarde a parke, enclosed with a wal
In compas rounde; and by a gate smal,
Who-so that wolde, frely myghte goon
Into this parke, walled with grene stoon.

And in I went to her the briddes songe,
Which on the braunches, bothe in pleyn and vale,
So loude songe that all the wode ronge,
Lyke as hyt sholde shever in pesis smale;
And as me thoghte that the nyghtyngale
Wyth so grete myght her voys gan out wrest[7],
Ryght as her hert for love wolde brest.[8]

The soyle was pleyn, smothe, and wonder softe,
Al over-sprad wyth tapites[9] that Nature
Had made her-selfe, celured[10] eke alofte
With bowys grene, the floures for to cure[11],
That in her beaute they may not longe endure
Fro al assaute of Phebus fervent fere[12],
Which in his spere so hote shone, and clere.

(22–56)

The great achievement of this passage is one of literary syn-
thesis, for it is essentially an interweaving of Chaucerian and
other images, phrases and ideas into a decorative pattern

[1] balm.   [2] began.   [3] abroad, openly.   [4] gold-burnished.
[5] sphere.   [6] skirt, follow.   [7] force, strain.   [8] burst.   [9] carpets.
[10] canopied.   [11] protect.   [12] fire.

with a beauty of its own. It is the pattern that matters, for
the tendency of the description is always from physical concretion and towards abstract truth. The imagery, for instance, relates the natural objects always to human artefacts,
to precious stones and jewels, or to decorative cloths, and the
textures are not natural but artificial textures—the trees in
the wood seem to be made of fragile china. Behind this
'humanization' of nature lies the medieval view of nature
as essentially meaningless except in a context of human ideas.
The physical world is an image of order, decorum and
design, as we see in the account of the ordered functions of
Titan and Nature herself. In the *Troy-book* this philosophical quality, the sense of ordered cyclic progression, is brought
out very strongly in the many fine passages of nature description which punctuate the narrative, and provides an effective
counterpoint to the fluctuations of human fortune.

The passage from the *Black Knight* is thus fundamentally
non-representational, and its truth is not one of physical
quality or texture or movement but inner and abstract.
The world of sensuous reality is patterned out of existence,
and in the pattern is established the *stasis* to which all Lydgate's poetry draws, and in which the uncomfortable contra-
dictions of experience are eliminated. Lydgate may have
seen the dawn many times, but when he describes it he does
not describe what he has seen:

> The nyght ypassed, at spryngyng of the day,
> Whan that the larke with a blissed lay
> Gan to salue the lusty rowes[1] rede
> Of Phebus char[2], that so freschely sprede
> Upon the bordure of the orient.
>
> (*Troy* I. 1,197–1,201)

The poet's job is not to describe 'real' dawns, which you can
see for yourself if you want to, but to draw out the metaphysical reality of dawn, and this is done in terms of decorative art—the chariot of Phebus with its stylized red rays,

---

[1] rays.   [2] chariot.

which would have been familiar to the medieval audience from their calendars and books of hours, and which would have reminded them of the ordered governance of the world:

That the world with stable feyth varieth accordable chaungynges; that the contrarious qualities of elementz holden among hemself ally-aunce perdurable; that Phebus, 'the sonne, with his goldene chariet bryngeth forth the rosene day; that the moone hath comaundement over the nyghtes ... al this accordaunce of thynges is bounde with love, that governeth erthe and see, and hath also comandement to the hevene.

(Boethius, Book II, metre 8, Chaucer's translation)

Just as Lydgate's style is rhetorical, oriented towards conventional figural decoration, so his world is rhetorical, one in which the material of experience yields, through the filter of a purely literary and non-experiential imagination, a series of conventional types and themes.

The futility of looking in Lydgate for the kind of transcript of real experience we habitually look for in poetry is illustrated too by his description of persons, especially of women, as of the lady in the 'Temple of Glass',

> which right as the sonne
> Passeth the sterres and doth hir stremes donne,[1]
> And Lucifer, to voide the nyghtes sorow,
> In clerenes passeth erli bi the morow;
> And so as Mai hath the sovereinte
> Of evere moneth, of fairnes and beaute,
> And as the rose in swetnes and odoure
> Surmounteth floures, and bawme of al licour
> Haveth the pris[2], and as the rubie bright
> Of al stones in beaute and in sight,
> As it is know, hath the regalie[3]:
> Right so this ladi with hir goodli eighe,[4]
> And with the stremes of hir loke so bright,
> Surmounteth all thurugh beaute in my sighte:
> Forto tel hir gret semelines,
> Hir womanhed, hir port,[5] and hir fairnes,
> It was a mervaile, hou ever that nature

[1] make pale.   [2] prize.   [3] supremacy.   [4] eyes.   [5] bearing.

> Coude in his werkis make a creature
> So aungel like, so goodli on to se,
> So femynyn or passing of beaute . . .

> (251–70)

The description continues in the same vein for many lines, as if to demonstrate that Lydgate could go on for ever without mentioning a single detail of the lady's appearance. Nearly all medieval description is rhetorically idealizing—even the Pilgrims in the General Prologue, we remember, are usually supreme in their chosen profession—but it is specially characteristic of Lydgate to move away so consistently and systematically from individuation and concretion towards the metaphysical abstract of generalized truth. The description, and it is the model for many similar descriptions, including one of over a hundred lines in the 'Flower of Courtesy', is not of a woman, but of womanliness.

The passage above demonstrates how closely the rhetorical ideal of amplification is wedded to Lydgate's characteristic ordering of reality in terms of non-descriptive abstraction. The technique there is one of extended metaphorical analogy, but there are other techniques of idealization, and they are amongst Lydgate's most readily recognizable stylistic habits. One technique is to assert his own inadequacy to the task:

> I am to rude her vertues everychone
> Cunnyngly to discryve and write. . . .
> ('Flower of Courtesy'. 176–7)

Lydgate's poetry is full of references to his having never gathered flowers in Tullius' garden, nor slept on Mount Citheron, nor drunk at the Well of Helicon, nor found favour with Calliope, having been born at Lydgate, 'Wher Bachus liquor doth ful scarsli flete' (*Fall* VIII. 194). Another technique is to declare that the full surpassing excellence of his theme would take too long to describe: 'A large boke it wolde occupie' (*Troy* III. 5,565). Another is to assert the essential inexpressibility of the theme:

> O, who can write a lamentacioun
> Convenient,[1], O Troye, for thi sake?
> Or who can now wepe or sorwe make,
> Thi grete meschef to compleyne and crie?
> Certes, I trowe nat olde Jeremye. . . .
> . . . nor thou Ezechiel . . . Nor Danyel. . . .
> Alle youre teris myghte nat suffise.
>
> (*Troy* IV.   7,054–82)

This passage goes on for fifty lines, and is one of many such where Lydgate expands his material in a typically 'literary' way. A fourth technique is by quotation of hitherto supreme exemplars of a particular virtue or passion which are now surpassed, as in the *topos* for the overwhelming grief of Helen for the dead Paris:

> I trowe that never man before
> No woman sawe falle in swiche distresse,
> In swiche disjoint of dedly hevines,
> Nor for no wo so pitously rave:
> Nat Cleopatre goynge to hir grave,
> Nor woful Tesbe, that from the kave sterte,
> Whan she hir silfe smote unto the herte,
> Nor the feithful trewe Orestille . . .
>
> (*Troy* IV.   3,654–61)

And so for another twenty lines. All these techniques are conventional, and it would be true to say that it is in the elaboration of the conventional, whether in theme or style, that Lydgate finds his truest home. He often has trouble organizing the intractable material of experience, and the things to be said so crowd upon him that his syntax bends and sinks beneath the pressure (Lydgate is one of the few writers who can produce sentences which lack not only a subject but a predicate too). But when he is secure in a familiar convention Lydgate can often attain a richness of expression which, although it is a richness produced by accumulation of quantity rather than density of quality, is one of his most characteristic achievements. The convention

---

[1] suitable.

seems to release what is best in him, not inhibit it, and no
better illustrations could be given than his 'Danse Macabre'
or his handling of the *Ubi sunt* formula in the magnificent
Envoy on Rome at the end of Book II of the *Fall*.

In the realm of action, Lydgate's technique, of systematically interpreting reality in terms of 'ideal' stereotypes, in-
volves the elimination of movement and development and
the substitution of static pictorial composition.   One of
Gower's gifts is to be able to catch the moment of significant
action—Medea kissing her maid in her excitement—but
Lydgate characteristically freezes the process of life into non-
physical abstraction.   This, for instance, is how he describes
Medea 'falling in love':

> Al sodeinly hir fresche rosen hewe
> Ful ofte tyme gan chaunge and renewe,
> An hondrid sythe in a litel space.
> For now the blood from hir goodly face
> Unto hir hert unwarly gan avale,[1]
> And therewithal sche wexe ded and pale;
> And efte anoon, who that can take hed,
> Hir hewe chaungeth into a goodly red.
> But evere amonge[2] t'ennwen[3] hir colour,
> The rose was meynt[4] with the lillie flour;
> And though the rose stoundemele[5] gan pase,
> Yit the lillie abideth in his place
> Til nature made hem efte to mete.
> And thus with colde and with sodein hete
> Was Medea in hir silfe assailled,
> And passyngly vexed and travailed,
> For now sche brent, and now sche gan to colde.
>
> (*Troy* I.   1,951–67)

Chaucer spends a thousand lines of his most glowing art on
this same movement of feeling in Criseyde, but for Lydgate,
it will be seen, all the complexities of human behaviour are
resolved into a remorselessly simple series of polarities.   The

---

[1] flow.   [2] ever and again.   [3] blend, shade off.   [4] mixed.
[5] from time to time.

familiar oxymoron of hot and cold is for him not a form of decoration merely, but actually takes the place of experiential material. Later, too, the conflict in Medea's heart, when she debates on love with herself, is expressed in terms of a similar mechanical series of abstractions:

> For in hir breste ther was atwixe tweyne
> A gret debate, and a stronge bataille,
> So fervently eche other dide assaile;
> And this contek[1], in ernest and no game,
> Juparted[2] was betwixe Love and Schame.
>
> (*Troy* I. 2,160–4)

This simple psychomachia is elaborated through another eighty-four lines, but there is no progress, no further penetration to the heart of the matter, only decoration and amplification of the given pattern. Comparison with Criseyde's soliloquy (*Troilus* II. 703–805) reveals the essential and profound difference between the poet responding imaginatively to the human situation and the rhetorician elaborating a thematic commonplace.

Perhaps of all his 'themes' the most frequently and elaborately developed is that of human duplicity, as in this account of Antenor's treachery:

> For undernethe he was with fraude fraught,
> This sleighti wolfe, til he his pray hath kaught;
> For he was clos and covert in his speche
> As a serpent, til he may do wreche,[3]
> Hydinge his venym under floures longe;
> And as a be, that stingeth with the tonge
> Whan he hath shad oute his hony sote,[4]
> —Sugre in the crop, venym in the rote—
> Right so, in soth, with tonge of scorpioun
> This Anthenor, rote of al tresoun,
> His tale tolde with a face pleyn,
> Liche the sonne that shyneth in the reyn,
> That faire sheweth though the weder be
> Wonder divers and troubly for to se.
>
> (*Troy* IV. 5,213–26)

---

[1] strife.   [2] put to the hazard.   [3] vengeance.   [4] sweet.

This same sequence of images is repeated, with variation and expansion, on at least twenty-five other occasions in Lydgate's poetry, and merges with another contrasting pattern of images expressive of universal mutability, the 'sorrow after joy' theme. The economy of imagery is indicative of the way all reality is channelled into a number of literary stereotypes, and of the way in which every subtle shade of human experience, every subtle blend of moral black and white, is programmed in binary terms through Lydgate's literary computer.

The fascination of Lydgate's style is endless, and to some extent self-sufficient, for there is no other poet in whom 'style' becomes so nearly an end in itself, a fixed entity, whose relation to 'subject' is one of abstract congruence not expressive embodiment. But the interest would be a superficial one if it were not part of a larger response to Lydgate's deeper patterns of meaning—not patterns of experience, for, as we have seen, experience is essentially meaningless to Lydgate, but moral and philosophical patterns. We may conclude with a survey of these larger aspects of Lydgate's achievement.

Humour is not something we think of very readily in connection with Lydgate, but there is one field in which a set moralistic assumption releases irony of a kind which is all the more delightful for its being unexpected, namely, the field of anti-feminist satire. Here Lydgate is in his element. In the *Troy-book*, whenever he comes to one of Guido's many diatribes against women, he prepares for it elaborately with apologies and disclaimers of responsibility and then translates the offending passage with evident relish and skilful embellishment, ending with further excuses and disingenuous offers of defence, such as that if women are by nature bad, then they can hardly be blamed for following their nature. The irony is never delicate, but it is sharp, and it hits home. Throughout the *Fall* too, the subject is one which arouses his keenest interest: he expands with great verve and brilliance Boccaccio's famous Juvenalian attack

upon women (I. 6,511), and makes a new interpretation of
the Orpheus-story as an allegory of the hell of marriage:

> But who hath onys infernal peynys seyn,
> Will never his thankis[1] come in the snare ageyn.
>
> (*Fall* I. 5,830–1)

There is elaborate ironical treatment of women also in
'Reason and Sensuality' and in the shorter poems (e.g.
'Bycorne and Chichevache', 'Beware of Doubleness', 'Horns
Away'), which have, as has been said, a pithy pungency and
wit which we do not usually associate with Lydgate.

The irony here is clearly drawn from a moral commonplace, and it is in terms of the eloquent elucidation of moral
commonplaces that we must see Lydgate's poetry. He has
also, for instance, deep and enduring political concerns. The
Troy-book is something of a 'Mirour for Princes' in its analysis of political morality, and the *Fall* returns again and again
to persistent themes: the evil of dissension amongst princes,
the dangers of false succession, the reliance of lordship on the
love of the people, and the necessity of personal integrity to
good government. The themes are familiar, but they had a
pressing relevance to the troubled and divided England of
Lydgate's day, and they are handled with sombre eloquence.
Perhaps the most overtly political of his longer poems is the
Siege of Thebes, which uses the classical story as a text for a
debate on war and peace which must have seemed very
pointed in the last years of Henry V's reign, when the con-
tinuance of the French wars was a burning issue.

In matters of love, too, Lydgate's approach, as one might
expect, is essentially moralistic. The portrait of the lover's
service which he gives in the 'Black Knight' and the 'Temple
of Glass' is one in which duty subsumes all passion, and in
which the exercise of virtue in love is made the precise ana-
logue of virtue in general. The resemblance to Gower is
close, but Lydgate's development of the doctrine is far more
lofty and serious, as well as more attenuated, than Gower's.

[1] willingly.

When he is writing within a strict formal tradition, as in the 'Complaints' in the two poems, his imagination can produce, from the traditional apparatus of image, conceit and classical allusion, a richness of order which is perfectly correspondent to his vision of life, a crystalline vision purged of the taint of earth. Lydgate's psychology of love is of the simplest, and is quite satisfied with arrows and wounds, but his expression of the perfectly refined ideal and doctrine of love has something that we might call moral fervour, though it is never transcendental.

It is, however, in the field of Boethian morality that Lydgate is most at home, and writes best. The *Troy-book* has many qualities—it is indeed the cornerstone of Lydgate's achievement—but its enduring effect upon the reader is in its solemn, moving and deeply eloquent exposition of the great platitudes of human experience—the punishment of sin, the transitoriness of earthly happiness and the falseness of earthly fame, the mutability of Fortune, and the inevitability of death. He may have begun the poem as a chivalric exemplar, but, as he wrote, his imagination was stirred to a contemplation of the story as a tragic text for the universal predicament, and he rises to the theme with the full power of his rhetoric in such passages as the lament for Troy in Book IV. The *Fall* too is like an enormous Epilogue, or Envoy on Fame, and has moments, despite its central artistic incoherence, of even greater grandeur, when Lydgate is moved by something like tragic moral vision. The work as a whole is a dark panorama of universal history, held from chaos by the persistence and integrity of Lydgate's moral patterning.

Of Lydgate's religious poetry we have said little, though we might expect that it would be the heart of his achievement. For the most part he gives to it a different kind of attention, in which rhetoric is heightened beyond language into liturgical ritual. There are a number of religious poems in which he speaks out of a simpler religious feeling, in particular the 'Testament', though it would be a mistake to treat this poem as autobiographical in any but the most con-

ventionalised sense, since self-expression would be as foreign
to Lydgate's idiom as self-consciousness. The last stanza is
justly famous, though it is not in a manner which we can
regard as characteristic of Lydgate:

> Tarye no lenger toward thyn herytage,
> Hast on thy weye and be of ryght good chere,
> Go eche day onward on thy pilgrimage,
> Thynke howe short tyme thou hast abyden here;
> Thy place is bygged[1] above the sterres clere,
> Noon erthly palys wrought in so statly wyse.
> Kome on, my frend, my brother most entere!
> For the I offered my blood in sacryfice.
>
> ('Testament'.   890–7)

Totally characteristic of Lydgate, however, is the 'Life of
Our Lady', a rich anthology of Marian themes in which
Lydgate's devotional intensity achieves perfect poetic expression. The best writing is in the most formal passages, such
as that on the Conception, in which the exuberance of the
Marian imagery is lavishly displayed, but above all in the
Prologue, where the traditional images of *stella maris* and
flos campi blend into a vision of the Virgin's birth as the
dawning of day upon the world's night. Familiar material
is here exploited, through Lydgate's luminous rhetoric, with
transfiguring effect, and it would not be too much to call this
one of the finest passages of non-personal religious poetry in
English.

---

[1] built.

GOWER AND LYDGATE

A Select Bibliography

(Place of publication, London, unless stated otherwise)

Bibliography

A MANUAL OF THE WRITINGS IN MIDDLE ENGLISH 1050–1400, by J. E. Wells. With Supplements to 1945; Yale, (1916)
—a new edition is in progress.

A BIBLIOGRAPHY OF 15TH CENTURY LITERATURE, by L. L. Tucker and A. R. Benham; Seattle (1928).

GUIDE TO ENGLISH LITERATURE: FROM BEOWULF THROUGH CHAUCER AND MEDIEVAL DRAMA, by D. M. Zesmer. With Bibliography by S.B. Greenfield; New York, (1961).

General Works: Literary, Cultural and Historical Background

AUREATE TERMS, by J. C. Mendenhall; Philadelphia (1919).

THE WANING OF THE MIDDLE AGES, by J. Huizinga (1924)
—rich and suggestive survey of continental cultural background.

DER ENGLISCHE FRUHHUMANISMUS: EIN BEITRAG ZUR ENGLISCHEN LITERATURGESCHICHTE DES 15. JAHRHUNDERTS, by W. F. Schirmer; Leipzig (1931).

THE THREE ESTATES IN MEDIEVAL AND RENAISSANCE LITERATURE, by Ruth Mohl; New York (1933).

POETIC DICTION IN THE ENGLISH RENAISSANCE, by V. L. Rubel; New York (1941).

ENGLISH LITERARY CRITICISM: THE MEDIEVAL PHASE, by J. W. H. Atkins; Cambridge (1943).

THE CROOKED RIB: AN ANALYTICAL INDEX TO THE ARGUMENT ABOUT WOMEN IN ENGLISH AND SCOTS LITERATURE TO 1568, by F. L. Utley; Ohio (1944).

FROM SCRIPT TO PRINT: AN INTRODUCTION TO MEDIEVAL LITERATURE, by H. J. Chaytor; Cambridge (1945).

'Medieval Literature and the Modern Reader', by H. S. Bennett, *Essays and Studies*, XXXI (1946).

ENGLISH ART 1307–1461, by Joan Evans; Oxford (1949).

THE SEVEN DEADLY SINS, by M. W. Bloomfield; Michigan State College Press (1952).

43

EUROPEAN LITERATURE AND THE LATIN MIDDLE AGES, by E. R. Curtius, trans. W. R. Trask; New York (1953)
—a work of fundamental importance for the study of all medieval literature.

SECULAR LYRICS OF THE XIVTH AND XVTH CENTURIES, ed. R. H. Robbins; Oxford (1955).

COMPLAINT AND SATIRE IN EARLY ENGLISH LITERATURE, by J. Peter; Oxford (1956)
—especially chapters iii and iv.

HUMANISM IN ENGLAND DURING THE 15TH CENTURY, by R. Weiss, 2nd ed.; Oxford (1957).

MEDIEVAL ENGLAND, ed. A. L. Poole, 2 vols; Oxford (1958).

THE FOURTEENTH CENTURY 1307–1399, by May McKisack; Oxford (1959).

HISTORICAL POEMS OF THE XIVTH AND XVTH CENTURIES, ed. R. H. Robbins; Oxford (1959).

THE INDIAN SUMMER OF ENGLISH CHIVALRY, by A. B. Ferguson; Durham, North Carolina (1960).

THE FIFTEENTH CENTURY 1399–1485, by E. F. Jacob; Oxford (1961).

LITERATURE AND PULPIT IN MEDIEVAL ENGLAND, by G. R. Owst, 2nd ed.; Oxford (1961)
—authoritative survey of the influence of preaching on literature.

THE ROMANCE OF THE ROSE, trans. H. W. Robbins (1962)
—an effective translation of a pervasively influential poem.

THE COURT OF RICHARD II, by G. Mathew (1968).

JOHN GOWER

Editions and Translations

THE COMPLETE WORKS OF JOHN GOWER, ed. G. C. Macaulay, in 4 vols: Vol. I, French Works; Vols II and III, English Works; Vol. IV, Latin Works; Oxford (1899–1902)
—the standard edition. Indispensable.

FOURTEENTH CENTURY VERSE AND PROSE, ed. K. Sisam; Oxford (1921)
—extract xii presents Gower's stories of Ceix and Alceone (IV. 2927–3123) and Adrian and Bardus (V. 4937–5162), well edited.

THE MAJOR LATIN WORKS OF JOHN GOWER, translated E. W. Stockton; Seattle (1962)
—valuable Introduction to all the non-English works.

JOHN GOWER, CONFESSIO AMANTIS (THE LOVER'S SHRIFT), translated into modern English verse by Terence Tiller (1963)
—translation, fluent and generally accurate, is of excerpts (about 8000 lines) linked by prose summary. The cutting is fickle and arbitrary. The introduction is not always reliable.

CONFESSIO AMANTIS, ed. R. A. Peck; New York (1968) about half the poem, in well-chosen extracts.

Studies

ESSAYS ON MEDIEVAL LITERATURE, by W. P. Ker (1905)
—useful essay on Gower, p. 101.

COURTLY LOVE IN CHAUCER AND GOWER, by W. G. Dodd, Harvard Studies in English, I, (1913)
—a standard survey.

THE ALLEGORY OF LOVE, by C. S. Lewis; Oxford (1936)
—Perceptive and affectionate appreciation, see pp. 198–222.

'Chaucer's Man of Law as a Literary Critic', by W. L. Sullivan, Modern Language Notes, LVIII, 1953
—Chaucer and Gower.

STUDIEN ZU JOHN GOWER, by Maria Wickert; Köln (1953)
—mostly on the Vox Clamantis; one chapter on the Confessio.

'John Gower, Mentor for Royalty: Richard II' by G. R. Coffman, Publications of the Modern Language Association of America, LXIX, 1954.

'The Poet in John Gower', by P. Fison, Essays in Criticism, VIII (1958)
—a slight but pleasant essay.

'John Gower's Confessio Amantis and the first Discussion of Rhetoric in the English Language', by J. J. Murphy, Philological Quarterly, XLI, 1962.

'The Manciple's Tale: Parody and Critique', by R. Hazelton, Journal of English and Germanic Philology, LXII, 1963
—finds 'satire' on Gower.

ANGLO-NORMAN LITERATURE AND ITS BACKGROUND, by M. Dominica Legge; Oxford (1963)
—on the French poems.

JOHN GOWER: MORAL PHILOSOPHER AND FRIEND OF CHAUCER, by J. H. Fisher; New York (1964)
—likely to remain the standard work on Gower for many years.

'Gower's Narrative Art', by D. Pearsall, *Publications of the Modern Language Association of America*, LXXXI, 1966.

PATTERNS OF LOVE AND COURTESY: Essays in memory of C. S. Lewis, ed. J. Lawlor (1966)

—essays on Gower by J. A. W. Bennett and J. Lawlor.

Source-Study

OVID: METAMORPHOSES, trans. F. J. Miller, 2 vols (1916); FASTI, trans. J. G. Frazer (1931); HEROIDES and AMORES, trans. G. Showerman (1914). Loeb Classical Library

—for study of Gower's handling of a major source.

SOURCES AND ANALOGUES OF CHAUCER'S CANTERBURY TALES, ed. W. F. Bryan and Germaine Dempster; Chicago (1941)

—for comparison of Chaucer and Gower in their use of the same material.

SHAKESPEARE: PERICLES PRINCE OF TYRE

—for comparison with Gower's *Apollonius of Tyre* (not Shakespeare's source).

JOHN LYDGATE

Editions:

Most of Lydgate's works are edited for the Early English Text Society, Extra Series. The major texts are as follows:

FALL OF PRINCES, ed. H. Bergen (Nos. 121-4, 1924-7); TROY-BOOK, ed. H. Bergen (97, 103, 106, 126, 1906-35); SIEGE OF THEBES, ed. A. Erdmann and E. Erkwall (108, 125, 1911-30); PILGRIMAGE OF THE LIFE OF MAN, ed. F. J. Furnivall and K. Locock (77, 83, 92, 1899-1904); REASON AND SENSUALITY, ed. E. Sieper (84, 89, 1901-3); TEMPLE OF GLASS, ed. J. Schick (60, 1891)—important introduction; MINOR POEMS, ed. H. N. MacCracken (107, 192, 1911-34)—study of Lydgate canon in Vol. I.

Other Texts:

ST EDMUND AND FREMUND, ed. C. Horstmann (*Altenglische Legenden*, 1881).

 THE LYFE OF ST ALBON AND ST AMPHABEL, ed. C. Horstmann (*Festschrift der Realschule zu Berlin*, 1882).

LIFE OF OUR LADY, ed. J. A. Lauritis, R. A. Klinefelter and V. F. Gallagher (*Duquesne Studies, Philological Series*, 2, Pittsburgh, 1961).

Studies:

ENGLISH VERSE BETWEEN CHAUCER AND SURREY, ed. Eleanor P. Hammond; Durham, North Carolina (1927)
—see pp. 77–187, extensive selections from Lydgate, with an excellent introduction: much the best criticism to date. The whole book is invaluable.

THE ALLEGORY OF LOVE, by C. S. Lewis; Oxford (1936)
—pp. 239–43, on the love-poems.

CHAUCER AND THE FIFTEENTH CENTURY, by H. S. Bennett; Oxford (1947)
—standard literary-historical survey of the English Chaucerians

'Lydgate's "Halff Chongyd Latyne"': an Illustration', by Isabel Hyde, *Modern Language Notes*, LXX, 1955.
—examples of Lydgate's Latinized diction.

'Medieval History, Moral Purpose, and the Structure of Lydgate's *Siege of Thebes*', by R. W. Ayers, *Publications of the Modern Language Association of America*, LXXIII, 1958.

JOHN LYDGATE: A STUDY IN THE CULTURE OF THE XVTH CENTURY, by W. F. Schirmer, trans. Ann E. Keep (1961)
—a thorough and careful study of the whole range of Lydgate's work and its background.

'Attitudes towards Women in Lydgate's Poetry', by A. Renoir, *English Studies*, XLII, 1961.

'Lydgate's Metaphors', by J. Norton Smith, *English Studies*, XLII, 1961.

JOHN LYDGATE: POEMS, ed. J. Norton-Smith; Oxford (1966)
—valuable anthology, with full apparatus.

CHAUCER AND CHAUCERIANS, ed. D. S. Brewer (1966)
—includes 'The English Chaucerians', by D. Pearsall, pp. 201-39.

THE POETRY OF JOHN LYDGATE, by A. Renoir (1967).

THE ENGLISH RELIGIOUS LYRIC IN THE MIDDLE AGES, by R. Woolf; Oxford (1968).